MOMENTS TO LIVE BY—
YEARS TO ENJOY

Kermit R. Carr

VANTAGE PRESS
New York / Washington / Atlanta
Los Angeles / Chicago

Illustrated Ken Landgraf

FIRST EDITION

All rights reserved, including the right of
reproduction in whole or in part in any form.

Copyright © 1987 by Kermit R. Carr

Published by Vantage Press, Inc.
516 West 34th Street, New York, New York 10001

Manufactured in the United States of America
ISBN: 0-533-06945-9

Library of Congress Catalog Card No.: 85-91430

*Moments to Live By—
Years to Enjoy*

To those who appreciate
inspirational, devotional, challenging messages

Preface

Several years ago, I wrote, produced and narrated a radio program titled, "Moments to Live By." At that time, almost all the programs on the air on Sunday morning were highly commercialized and the music was secular; none identified with the Sabbath. "Moments to Live By" was designed to enhance one's appreciation and enjoyment of the Sabbath. (There were no commercials). The message that preceded each song that was played helped motivate each listener to broaden his knowledge and to understand the meaning of each song. This book represents a collection of one hundred Sunday "Moments to Live By." These introduction to songs should be excitingly refreshing and should serve to enrich one's daily life. I hope you enjoy the messages as much as I enjoyed writing them. May God bless you as you read and apply the inspiring messages to your daily living.

Introduction

Enrich your life. . . . In a troubled world, you will find a refreshing alternative in . . . Moments to Live By—Years to Enjoy.

One day long, long ago I was walking down **The Kings Highway** and saw **The Footprints of Jesus** and in the distance **The Old Rugged Cross.** I was troubled, very troubled. Why did I feel as though I had been lost **Ten Thousand Years** and that they had been **Wasted Years.** Suddenly, I **Met the Master.** I immediately fell to my knees and pleaded, "**Help Me, Lord,** have **Mercy** on me!" The skies opened up and **Heaven Came Down and Glory Filled My Soul.** I cried out, "Dear Lord, **You Have Give Life to Me!**" Then and there I knew that I was on **The Road That Leads to Heaven** and that I was **Sheltered in the Arms of God!** As I felt the gentle breezes blowing against my uplifted face, I realized that **Even the Winds Whisper His Name.**

Somehow, I knew He would **Release Me from My Sin** and that I would experience **Peace in the Valley** of my life. "**I Won't Ask for More,**" I promised, "because now **I Am Thine, Oh Lord,** your **Love Lifted Me.**" Yet I was compelled to ask, "**Why Me, Lord?**" When **I Looked Up and He Looked Down,** I knew the answer: **Love Is Why. Love is the Key,** and Christ holds **The Keys to the Kingdom. He Chose to Live in Me** and fill my life with **Sunshine and Roses** Because **He Cares.** I whispered, "**Thank You, Lord, for Loving Me!**"

Since He Touched Me, I have been **Born Again.** Now that I am **Learning to Lean on Jesus,** I recognize that **Christ Is My Sunshine** and **Where He Leads Me** I will follow. Regardless of how much the skeptics try to discredit Him or consider Him just a myth, I know that **My God Is Real** and **He's Alive** and **Something Beautiful. Because He Lives** and because He keeps my heart and life in tune, I can face tomorrows with a song in my heart.

When I have **Just a Little Talk with Jesus in the Garden, On the Jerico Road,** or as I worship in **The Church in the Wildwood,** I am resolved to **Rise Again** and tell the whole wide world that I'm **Standing on the Solid Rock** where I can see **Treasures Unseen** before. Now that I have Christ's **Blessed Assurance, Gone** is my world of worry, apprehension, and anxiety.

Because **I'm on My Way to Heaven, It Is No Secret** that I'm **Feeling Better All the Time,** and life gets **Sweeter as the Days Go By.** I wanted **Someone To Care,** and when I felt **The Touch of the Master's Hand,** I knew that **Jesus Was the One** and he **Will Hold My Hand.** When I say, **"Jesus, I Believe What You Say,"** I am voicing my conviction that **When the Savior Reached Down for Me, He Didn't Lift Me Up to Let Me Down.** It is refreshing to know that **My Lord is Always Near!**

Yes, **I Am Depending on Jesus. Jesus Fills My Every Need,** and I know that **I Can Call on Jesus Anytime! The Love Of God** is so real . . . so deep and far-reaching . . . so satisfying . . . so comforting . . . so wonderful and eternal, I want to stand on the mountaintop and shout to the whole wide world, **"Let's Just Praise Him** as we serve Him!"

I humbly ask Him to "Remind me, dear Lord, to take **Time to Be Holy** and to live **One Day at a Time."** I know **He's Got the Whole World in His Hands,** and although I may be surrounded by a host of friends, relatives, and loved ones, **No**

One Cares for Me like Jesus. He has a **Mansion Over the Hilltop** waiting for me, and **Heaven's Sounding Sweeter All the Time!**

"I want to promise you, dear Lord, that it's **Not My Will** but Thine be done, and let me take **Just a Closer Walk with Thee.** Please hold me close **Until the Storm Passes By."** When I lift my eyes toward Heaven and exclaim, **"How Great Thou Art!"** I envision the day **When They Ring Those Golden Bells** for me. I know **He Looked Beyond My Faults,** and **Though My Sins Be as Scarlet,** He will take me **Just as I Am** . . . and **What a Day That Will Be!**

Hallelujah!

*Moments to Live By—
Years to Enjoy*

PART I

How Great Thou Art! 3
All the Way 4
At Calvary 5
Beautiful Garden of Prayer 6
A Blue Christmas 7
Depending on Jesus 8
Do You Know Jesus?—Everybody Ought to Know Jesus 9
Do You Know Jesus?—Everybody Ought to Know Jesus 10
Everybody Ought to Know Jesus 11
God Is My Friend 12
He Knows Just How Much You Can Bear 13
He Knows Just What I Need 14
He Will Show You the Way 15
He's Everywhere 16
He's Everywhere 17
His Hand In Mine 18

How Great Thou Art!

It is possible—and I definitely hope it is probable—that everyone reading *Moments to Live By—Years to Enjoy* is busy getting ready to go to the church of his choice, to rededicate himself to a richer life through sincere worship and by living according to the principles laid down in the Ten Commandments. *Moments to Live By* was designed to help enhance your appreciation and enjoyment of this Sabbath Day! This is the day of all days when we lift our eyes toward Heaven and say to God, "How great Thou art!"

All the Way

Have you ever heard of "fair-weather friends"? When the sun is shining in your life, they are all around you. . . . They will go with you so long as you are a bright spot in their lives . . . but when the storm clouds begin to appear, it is sometimes difficult to find them. . . . Some are even hard to locate when only a small cloud drifts by. It is not hard to determine who your real friends are when a crisis comes into your life. Some who you thought would stand by your side all the way will disappear, but there is one who will stay with you till the end of time. I need not tell you that Jesus is not a "fair-weather friend." He will be with you regardless of the storms of strife. He will be with you when troubles come with tornado force . . . when hurricanes of disaster blow against you . . . and when cyclones twist your life. He will be with you not just for the duration of the storm, but he will be with you all the way!

At Calvary

Although we sometimes think otherwise, I can assure you that there's a cross for everyone to bear. But we should be thankful that there's a Heaven for each soul to share. I feel . . . and I know . . . there's a place in Heaven waiting for me. But I did not earn it. . . . I did not buy it. . . . No person gave it to me. I got it through Christ's death at Calvary. I realize that each drop of his blood bought me a million years . . . and a soul was born each time he shed a tear. In those times when I am inclined to feel important . . . when I try to give myself credit for what I am and what I will be in the eternity, I suddenly stop . . . and come face to face with the realization that He bought my soul at Calvary!

Are we worth the price?

Beautiful Garden of Prayer

Gardens are fascinating places. . . . The garden my mother used to have near our house. . . . Gardens like that of my neighbor who grows such delicious vegetables. . . . Gardens full of flowers—all types of flowers. In Charleston, South Carolina, there is a beautiful garden of flowers called Magnolia Gardens. People from hundreds—yes, even thousands—of miles away come to drink in the beauty of that garden. Throughout the United States and the world, we find beautiful gardens that capture our interest and contribute tremendously to our enjoyment of the beautiful things in life. There is another garden that occupies a memorable and meaningful place in our lives . . . in our history. And that is the Garden of Gethsemene. But the garden that keeps us closest to God—keeps us in touch with eternity—is the Beautiful Garden of Prayer. Let us enjoy that garden every day.

A Blue Christmas

I don't want anyone to have a blue Christmas this Christmas. . . . I want it to be a bright and shining Christmas for you—

> If I could do whate'er I want to do
> To make complete your gladsome Christmas Day,
> I would not bring a single thing to you,
> But I would come and take some things away.
>
> I'd take away all troubles from your heart,
> Each pain and sorrow I would have relieved,
> And every word that caused a single smart,
> And every hour through which you sadly grieved.
>
> I'd have them all be gone—forever gone—
> Forgotten, like the things that cannot be;
> And then each hour would be a joyful one,
> For only good things would be left, you see.
>
> Now that is what I'd really like to do—
> If I could do the things I wish for you.
>
> And, of course, I would take from you
> > A blue Christmas.

Depending on Jesus

Although the current trend is to look to the government for everything; nations of the world are looking to the United Nations to solve their problems and to the United States to furnish them with money, food, clothing . . . I look to God for everything I need upon this earth: my shelter, food, and clothing—in fact, whatever I am worth. Castro thinks he will be stronger if Cuba unites with the Soviet Union. The people of South Africa wonder to whom they should turn, the United States or the Soviet Union, for their strength. As far as I am concerned personally, I cannot ever be the least bit stronger than the strength my God has given me and no nation is going to be stronger than its loyalty to God. For my existence and subsistence I am not depending on the United States, the national government, not even my own country. I am depending on Jesus for everything I need, including inspiration for . . . my every word and deed. . . . I hope you will join me in depending on Jesus.

Do You Know Jesus?—
Everybody Ought to Know Jesus

A small, ragged, emaciated boy was kneeling in the snow-filled corner of a building, shivering from the cold wintry wind. His eyes were lifted toward Heaven, and you could hear him repeating the letters of the alphabet. When asked what he was doing, he replied, "My father and mother are dead. . . . My only sister lies in a cold room too sick . . . too hungry . . . too weak . . . too cold to get up from the pallet on the floor. We have no food . . . no heat . . . no medicine. I don't know any prayer, but I do know God, and I know that if I say the alphabet, God will know what's in my heart and He will spell out the prayer for me." What wonderful faith and knowledge! That little boy possessed life's greatest treasure. That little boy knew Jesus. Do you know Jesus? Don't you think everybody ought to know Jesus?

Do You Know Jesus?—
Everybody Ought to Know Jesus

The doctor knows his medicine and uses that knowledge for humanity. . . . The lawyer knows his law and with that law helps to protect his clients and the public. . . . The banker knows his bank, what his bank can contribute to the development of the community, and how to meet the needs of his customers. . . . The insurance executive knows the value of planned security and shares that knowledge for a greater future for a greater America. . . . The merchant knows his wares and helps the buying public to get the best. . . . But does the Christian know Christ? . . . And is he telling others? . . . Do you know Jesus? . . . How well do you know him? . . . Are you passing that knowledge on that others may share the benefits and joys of Christianity? . . . Don't you think everybody ought to know?

Everybody Ought to Know Jesus

Here are some interesting . . . challenging . . . timely questions. Are we selfish with our religion? Do we want to keep it a secret? Do we want to hide our Christ from others? Or does our action indicate that we don't care for the other fellow? We go to church on Sunday. . . . We read our Bible. . . . We stand up and pray. . . . Some of us even go to prayer meeting. But the question is, how about the person who doesn't go to church? Does he know about those things? Does he know our Christ? Do we tell others about our Christian experience, our God, our Savior? Are we as proud of Christ and his kingdom as we are of our business . . . our family . . . our golf game . . . how many fish we caught . . . who won the football game . . . and on and on and on? Remember the command: "Go ye into all the world." That means our friends and neighbors as well as those in foreign lands. He has commissioned us to tell the story. There is no other way. Seriously, don't you think that everybody ought to know who Jesus is?

God Is My Friend

It has been said that a friend is someone who knows all about you yet is still your friend, someone you can tell your secrets to without fear of his betraying your confidence. A friend will stand by you when the sun is shining bright or when the sky is filled with storm clouds. There is a friend who will go with you all the way . . . who will always be near when you need him . . . who will be with you when your life is filled with laughter . . . or when you are burdened with the trials and tribulations of a hectic life. He is not a "fair weather friend," but someone who is ever by your side to lend a helping hand. He has never failed. . . . He never will. He has been tried and found to be true. I have had too many experiences not to recognize very easily and quickly that God is my friend.

He Knows Just How Much You Can Bear

Are you a chronic complainer? Are you one of those people who is always fussing about something? Do you sometimes feel, either genuinely or falsely, that the whole world has been dumped onto your lap or onto your back? I'm sure that there are many times in your life when your burdens seem just too much for you to bear and you ask, "Why did this have to happen to me? I just can't bear it. The burden is too much for me!" Remember this: The Bible teaches us that God will never give us a burden without giving us the strength to bear it. We have only to lean on Him. Give Him credit for being infinite . . . and there should be no question in your mind that He knows just how much you can bear!

He Knows Just What I Need

He came to my desk with a quivering lip—
    The lesson was done.
"Dear Teacher, I want a new leaf," he said,
    "I've spoiled this one."
I took the old leaf, stained and blotted,
And gave him a new one, all unspotted,
And into his sad eyes smiled.
    "Do better now, my child."

I went to the throne with a quivering soul—
    The year was done.
"Dear Father, hast Thou a new year for me?
    I've spoiled this one."
He took the old year, stained and blotted,
And gave me a new one, all unspotted,
And into my sad heart smiled.
    "Do better now, my child."

So I take this year 1986 and place it in His hands,
Because He knows just what I need.

He Will Show You the Way

The fugitive years follow each other on their appointed rounds. . . . Days and years are like the moods of men. . . . Some are full of sunshine and brightness, blue skies and the fragrance of flowers; others are gray with clouds and hints of rain and storm, fretfulness and complaining. . . . The New Year's young—just nine hours old—and it lies before us. . . . Let us not harbor the belief that we have plenty of time to make sure of our purposes. . . . Today alone is ours. . . . What we do today is the essential thing of our life. . . . Let us not waste any time. . . . Now is the hour—the minute—the moment—when we should surrender ourselves to God and let Him show us the way to a fuller, richer, more meaningful new year.

He's Everywhere

There has been a tendency through the years to place God somewhere up in the clouds, up in the sky, somewhere beyond the blue horizons, and leave Him there. But God is everywhere. He is the cry of a newborn babe . . . the drop of rain. He is the touch of a gentle breeze and the force of a tornado. We see Him in the rising sun . . . the twinkling stars. God is the snow on the mountains . . . the blue of the ocean's depths or a woman's eyes. In April's blossoms or crescent moon we see His majesty. He's in every flower that blooms and tree that grows. He's the beat of our heart . . . the air we breathe. Every living and beautiful thing reflects the presence of God. God is the author and finisher of all that is good. To anyone who can see . . . hear . . . smell . . . taste . . . feel. . . . He's everywhere!

He's Everywhere

I go to church on Sunday . . . and I say a fervent prayer . . . because I want the Lord to know . . . how much I really care. . . . Because I want to thank Him for . . . the blessings I have gained . . . not only in the sunshine, but . . . whenever it has rained. . . . And also to implore Him to . . . bestow the grace I need . . . to make myself presentable . . . in thought and word and deed . . . and tell him I am sorry for . . . the sinful side of me . . . and ask Him to forgive me for . . . my instability. . . . I go to church on Sunday for . . . the wonderful reward . . . of knowing that my heart and soul . . . are closer to the Lord.

We have developed a feeling that God is with us only on Sunday, that He's everywhere on Sunday, but the rest of the week He cannot be seen or heard or found. . . . Let us remind ourselves that on Monday, Tuesday, Wednesday, Thursday, Friday, and Saturday . . . we need to live for Him, because on these days, too, He's everywhere!

His Hand in Mine

You may ask me how I know my Lord is real,
    You may doubt the things I say and doubt the way I feel.
But I know God's real today; He'll always be,
    I can feel His hand in mine, and that's enough for me.

Other friends that I love so may pass me by.
    Other friends may never see the teardrops in my eye.
Other friends may never know the pain I bear;
    Every tear He wipes away and every heartache shares.

I will never walk alone. He holds my hand;
    He will guide every step I take, and if I fall I know He'll understand.
And when that time shall come to leave this world behind
    I'll walk that lonesome valley with His hand in mine!

PART II

I'd Rather Have Jesus than Silver or Gold   21
How Great Thou Art!   22
How Long Has It Been?   23
In Times like These We Need a Savior!   24
It Is No Secret   25
It's Wonderful!   26
It's Wonderful!   27
I Can Call Jesus Anytime   28
I'm Depending on Jesus   29
I'm Depending on Jesus   30
I Learned to Pray   31
I Need Thee Every Hour!   32
I Need Thee Every Hour!   33

I'd Rather Have Jesus than Silver or Gold

Almost every moment of every day we have to make decisions. And the decisions we make determine our future, both here and hereafter. The Scriptures say: "Choose you this day whom ye shall serve!" What is the most important thing in life to you? I think I can answer what *should* be the most important thing. But what do *you* consider the most important? Trays of silver . . . vaults of gold . . . business and political power . . . fame and popularity . . . social position? The components that make up this material world are perishable and have limited life and usefulness. I'm sure that our destiny could be assured if we could say with complete sincerity, "I'd rather have Jesus than silver or gold."

How Great Thou Art!

All around us we see evidence of God's handiwork. Even a tiny drop of rain can manifest the greatness of God. I marvel when the rain is drumming on my door . . . and on the windowpane . . . and on every corner of the house. . . . I hear its sad refrain. . . . It has a way of echoing . . . a melancholy sound. . . . Perhaps because it takes away . . . the sunshine all around. . . . And yet I know that it is meant . . . to make the flowers grow . . . and always it is needed for . . . the crops the farmers sow. It brings relief in summer, and . . . it washes off the street . . . and it provides a playground for . . . the children's naked feet. . . . And so I listen to it pour . . . and watch it drench the sod. . . . and welcome it because it is . . . the handiwork of God!

All that in a small drop of rain. Surely, when we look around and see all the things God has created, we can not help but raise our hearts toward Him and say, "How great Thou art!"

How Long Has It Been?

One Sunday morning I saw a man coming down the aisle of the church . . . wearing a broad and captivating smile. . . . I asked him, "Why the big smile?" He replied, "That is what you told me to do on your *Moments to Live By*, which I heard before I left home for Sunday school." And because of the many requests, I am repeating, word for word, the message I gave that Sunday . . . and will play the same song. . . . How long? How long has it been since you smiled . . . said a kind word to someone . . . since you thanked someone for doing a good job for your community . . . your church . . . your organization? . . . How long has it been since you have gone out of your way to do a kind deed? . . . How long has it been since you began the day with a smile? . . . Remember that your smile lights up the world awhile, that others feel cast down because they see your frown. . . . How long has it been since you attended church . . . made a contribution to your church . . . since you thanked the Lord for all he has done for you? . . . But the most important question this morning is, How long has it been since you talked to the Lord?

In Times like These We Need a Savior!

Whenever we see and listen to debates and speeches by the aspirants to the high office of president of the United States, we see the daily newspapers and read the headlines reporting waves of crime, including graft, murder and rape, violence, greed, strife . . . we shudder at the prospect of an atomic war . . . when daily we hear the threats of international gangsters and others who seek to destroy our great nation from within and from without, it is then we should realize more forcefully than ever that in times like these we need a savior!

It Is No Secret

The whole world is in a state of turmoil and strife. . . . The United States . . . Cuba . . . South America . . . The Congo . . . Europe . . . whenever the influence of the godless is felt there is strife. . . . In desperation, the nations turn to the United Nations for a solution . . . but no meeting of the United Nations can ever be the means of changing this world into a world of peace. . . . Yet something can be done. . . . "What? Is it a secret?" No—there is no secret. . . . First we must change the lives of individuals. . . . We must begin to think rightly, live rightly, according to the law of God, and peace will follow. . . . Once we find the Christ within, we will radiate that light to others and can change our home life . . . our occupational life . . . our community life and . . . eventually the lives of the nations. . . . It is no secret what God can do, and what He has done for others He can do for you . . . and what He can do for you He can do for the world. . . .

It's Wonderful!

When I arose this morning, my first thought was *It's wonderful to be alive! . . . To have the opportunity to begin a new day. . . .*

>Another dawn, another day,
>>Another chance, another way,
>To finish something I began
>>Or else to try another plan.

I said, "Thank you, Lord, for

>"Another day, another sun,
>>Another and a better one
>Another day I never had
>>Another reason to be glad!"

As I prepare to go to Sunday school and church, I find myself saying, "It's wonderful to live in a land where there is freedom of worship—where a person can worship according to the dictates of his heart." . . . The world is full of things that incite us to exclaim, "It's wonderful!" But when I think of God's love and how He gave His only begotten Son that we might inherit eternal life, I cannot help but say with renewed enthusiasm, "It's wonderful!"

It's Wonderful!

The world is full of wonders. We stand amazed at all that's happening today. We say the radio . . . TV . . . and new telephone system are wonderful achievements. . . . Our nation has made wonderful progress. . . . The setting sun and the rising sun present a wonderful view. . . . Love is a wonderful emotion. . . . This is a wonderful day in which to live. We refer to the Seven Wonders of the World . . . a trip beyond the moon, a wonderful experience. . . . It would be a wonderful blessing to have peace on earth and goodwill toward man. There are numerous synonyms that could be used as a substitute for the adjective *wonderful*, but when I think of the love of God and His compassion for me, I don't think anything can substitute for the expression "It's wonderful!"

I Can Call Jesus Anytime

When the ancients said, "A work well begun is half-done," they emphasized the importance of always endeavoring to make a good beginning. . . . With that thought in mind, I shall quote my New Year's resolution:

I will start anew this morning with a higher, fairer creed;
I will cease to stand complaining on my ruthless neighbor's greed;
I will cease to sit repining while my duty's call is clear;
I will waste no moment whining, and my heart shall know no fear.
I will look sometimes about me for the things that merit praise;
I will search for hidden beauties that elude the grumbler's gaze.
I will try to find contentment in the paths that I must tread;
I will cease to have resentment when another moves ahead.
I will not be swayed by envy when my rival's strength is shown;
I will not deny his merit, but I'll strive to prove my own;
I will try to see the beauty spread before me, rain or shine;
I will cease to preach your duty and be more concerned with mine.
—Author unknown

But I shall need strength and guidance as I seek to follow my New Year's resolution . . . so I turn to Jesus. . . . It is good to know that I can call Jesus anytime. . . .

I'm Depending on Jesus

Life is centered around depending on others. We cannot live isolated lives. Every moment of the day we depend on others. Someone for our food . . . our clothes . . . our homes . . . someone to educate our children . . . to doctor us. We can't do it by ourselves. And you may be surprised at how much people depend on you.

> So much depends on you
> On what you say or do,
> On every move you make
> And every step you take.
> You're only one, 'tis true,
> But much depends on you.
>
> Oh, you can every day
> Strew roses on life's way
> Or, if you choose, impart
> Deep sorrow in some heart.
> Be careful what you do,
> So much depends on you!

And when it comes to my eternal life, I have to be especially careful on whom I depend. I don't depend on my lawyer . . . my teacher . . . my banker . . . my doctor, not even my pastor. I'm depending on Jesus and He is depending on me.

I'm Depending on Jesus

I look to God for everything . . . I need upon this earth . . . My shelter, food, and clothing and . . . whatever I am worth. . . . Of course, I have to go to work . . . and do my certain share . . . and I must recognize my God . . . and tell Him that I care. But on the other hand I know . . . no matter what I do . . . I must depend upon my God . . . to help me see it through. . . . Because no matter how I try . . . I cannot ever be . . . the least bit stronger than the strength . . . my God has given me. . . . And that is why I look to God . . . for everything I need . . . including inspiration for . . . my every word and deed. If you have not already done so, why don't you, too, say, "I'm depending on Jesus!"

I Learned to Pray

There was a time when I was stooped with many burdens . . . burdens that I could not seem to bear. I looked everywhere for relief . . . for an answer to my dilemma. I talked to learned men. . . . I listened to the sages of my time. . . . I traveled, but nowhere could I find the answer. Nor did my burdens get any lighter. Everywhere I turned seemed to lead to more confusion. . . . That which I sought was always just beyond my grasp. What should I do? . . . Where should I turn? I asked myself a hundred—yea, thousands—of times. Then one day—like a ray of sunshine out of Heaven's blue—I found the answer—I learned to pray.

I Need Thee Every Hour!

Be with me, God, when I am glad . . . and all the skies are blue . . . and never let me fail to give . . . my gratitude to You. . . . Be with me when the night is dark . . . and the shadows cross my heart . . . that I may always keep the faith . . . and we'll never grow apart. . . . Let not my mind be lonely or . . . my footsteps go astray . . . but teach me how to live my life . . . according to Your way. . . . Be with me, God, when I am home . . . and when I travel far . . . and help me appreciate . . . the beauty of a star. . . . Be my companion everywhere . . . in happiness and tears. . . . Be with me, God, and give me grace . . . through all my earthly years.

    What I am really trying to say, Lord, is that I need thee every hour!

I Need Thee Every Hour!

When trouble comes into our lives, we find ourselves turning to someone for comfort . . . for help. We feel the need for someone. Normally, we need food three times each day, eight hours of sleep. We need to associate with people. . . . We need many hours of relaxation, so many hours for work and for diversion. But when deep sorrow comes into our heart, we suddenly feel the need for God. We turn to Him in prayer . . . in thought. But recognition of the need for God should not be a spontaneous thing—it should be permanent. When I am in sorrow, I need Him. . . . When the sun is shining in my life, I need him . . . rain or shine . . . cold or hot . . . night or day . . . in times of joy . . . in times of sorrow. . . . When I am tired or when I am rested . . . I need Him. Not just occasionally, but every hour of every day . . . I need Him! Let each of us turn to God and say with absolute sincerity, "I need Thee every hour!"

PART III

In My Father's House   37
In My Father's House   38
In My Father's House   39
In the Garden   40
In the Garden   41
Invisible Hands   42
Invisible Hands   43
I Won't Have to Cross Jordan Alone   44
If We Never Meet Again   45
I Found the Answer—I Learned to Pray   46
I Can Call Jesus Anytime   47
Jesus Fills Our Every Need   48
Jesus, I Believe What You Said!   49
Just a Closer Walk with Thee—the King and I   50

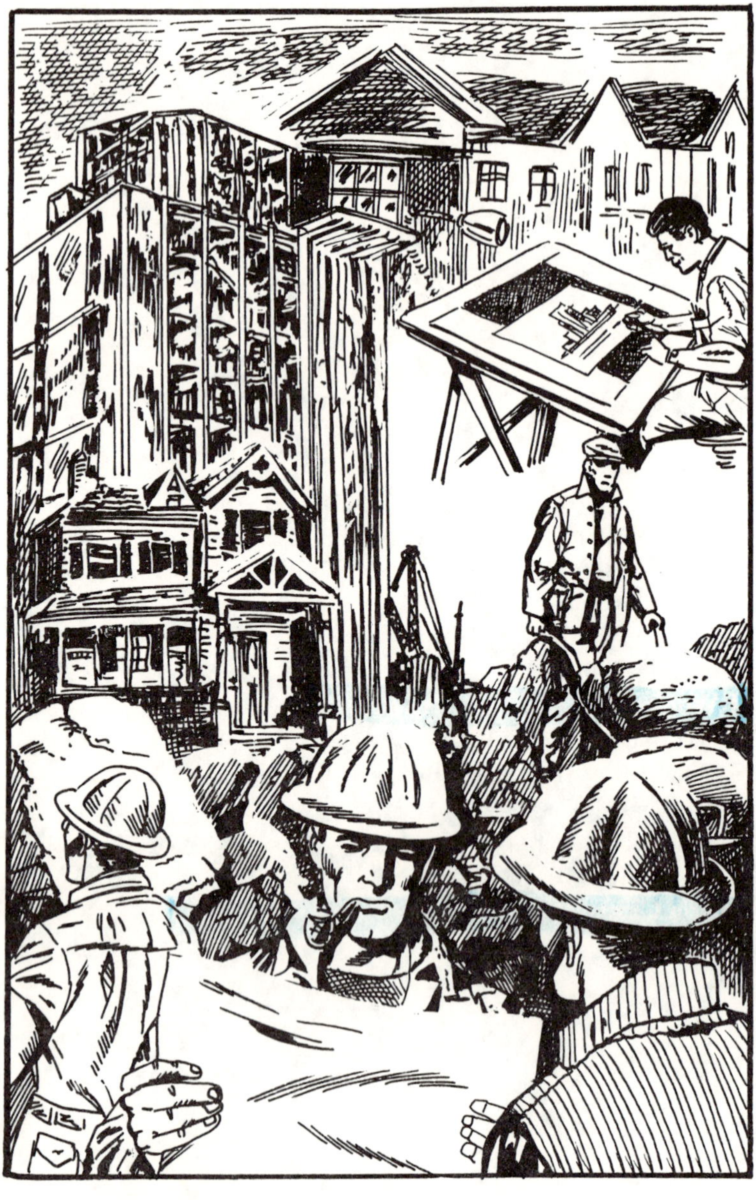

In My Father's House

We begin our program each Sunday morning with the biblical quotation "In my Father's house are many mansions," . . . and each morning I think of how the building trade is booming . . . and everywhere it seems . . . some architect is trying out . . . his home and office schemes. . . . I like to watch a structure rise . . . to beautify some place . . . or see an old establishment . . . take on a brighter face. . . . The movie, store, and restaurant . . . are practical and good . . . but homes are more important . . . to the growing neighborhood . . . and nothing like another house . . . appeals so much to me . . . because I know it will embrace . . . another family . . . because I know there will be love . . . and golden dreams to share . . . and happy children's laughter will be . . . echoing from there. And I think of how important it is for us to make a down payment on a home up there in our Father's house, where there are many mansions. And we must send along regular payments, too. We can't finish paying for it after we move in. We must have a clear title to the property; the home has to be paid for *before* we move in.

In My Father's House

Last Sunday morning when I was playing "In My Father's House Are Many Mansions," one of my listeners—a grand old man—sat down and wrote me a short letter. . . . Enclosed in that letter was a poem he had written about the *little guy*. . . . May I say to him, "No person who loves the Lord is a *little guy* . . . and that person will occupy a mansion up there by and by. . . ."

>Solitude and grim a sigh,
>But should I wonder or reason why?
>>I'm just a little guy.
>I've achieved not greatness with tongue and pen,
>And I don't stand abreast with the great amongst men.
>I'm beneath that estate in the toil and din—
>>I'm just a little guy.
>I don't travel far on what I get
>From efforts and work and toil and sweat,
>Tho I hope and trust and dream, yet
>>I'm still a little guy.
>Just a dreamer, I guess, 'twixt the love and hate
>Of the whims of the small and the deeds of the great.
>It's past noon for me—it may be too late
>>For this little guy.
>Yet I'll aim toward the love as I cherish the great,
>And I'll still strive to abide where I've banished all hate,
>And I'll walk a straight path that's uphill to a gate,
>Where there are mansions sublime for the good and the great.
>
>>But will a mansion I rate—or a cottage nearby?
>
>>I don't know. . . . I'm the little guy!

In My Father's House

At the beginning of this program I said, " 'In my Father's house are many mansions.' " We spend a lifetime building a home . . . down here . . . and I think we should. . . . Owning a home is one of life's great joys . . . whether it be a modest bungalow or a mansion in keeping with your income and standard of living. . . . But we must recognize this fact: Regardless of what type home we have here below, there will come a day when we will have to leave it. . . . As we make our monthly payments on our home down here, why not make daily payments on our mansions above? . . . In my Father's house are many mansions, but are we sending along the payments that will assure us a place there? May I suggest that we make our arrangements now—today—for sending our daily payments . . . which are made up of love, kindness, charity, faith, prayer, worship, forgiveness, loyalty to Christ . . . and many other types of payments? Yes, in my Father's house are many mansions. . . . Do you want to own the right kind of house in eternity? Why not make a down payment today on that home in your Father's house, where there are many mansions?

In the Garden

Back in my courtship days, I used to walk along lovers' lane . . . and I was thrilled as I held the hand of my true love. And before those wonderful days, I used to stroll through the woods—picking flowers, kicking stones, watching the birds and squirrels, and dabbling my feet in the cool waters of the springs. Many years have passed since those young and carefree days, but today I delight in those times when I can stroll down the street, through the woods, in the gardens with my granddaughter—I call her my great granddaughter, because she is great to me. She holds my hand and looks to me for safety, leadership, companionship. Yet I am ever conscious of another stroll I take, which touches my heartstrings and makes the greatest contribution to the abundance of my living . . . and that is when I walk in the garden with Him.

> And He walks with me, and He talks with me,
>   And He tells me I am His own.
>
> And the joy we share as we tarry there
>   None other has ever known!

In the Garden

Sometimes I walk in the shadows . . . sometimes in the clear sunlight. Sometimes I walk in the valley of despair or on the crest of a mountain. Other times I walk in the burning desert or wade in the cool waters. . . . I remember walking in green pastures when I was a child . . . also on land that was barren. I have walked where there was danger . . . and I have walked where there was peace and quiet. But the walks that have contributed most to my way of life and to my joy and comfort have been when I walked with Him in the garden.

>And He walks with me, and He talks with me,
>   And He tells me I am His own.
>
>And the joys we share as we tarry there
>   None other has ever known!

Invisible Hands

There is a hand that tills the soil . . . and gathers in the grain. . . . And one that serves the factory . . . or operates a train. . . . A hand that plays piano keys . . . or moves the pen to write. . . . And one that clasps in fond hello . . . or doubles up to fight. . . . There is a hand that leads a child . . . or stiffens in salute . . . that sweeps and scrubs and cooks the meals . . . or polishes a boot. . . . Yes, there are many human hands . . . according to their kind . . . and what they strive to say or do . . . and what they hope to find. . . . The hands that steal and plunder or . . . that beg for food each day . . . and those that close in love's embrace . . . or gently fold and pray.

    I place my hands in those of God . . . for it is His invisible hands that hold my tomorrows, my future.

Invisible Hands

I see his blood upon the rose
    And in the stars the glory of his eyes.
His body gleams amid eternal snows;
    His tears fall from the skies.

I see his face in every flower;
    The thunder and the singing of the birds
Are his voice—and craven by his power
    Rocks are his written words.

All pathways by his feet are worn;
    His strong heart stirs the ever beating sea.
His crown of thorns is twined with every thorn;
    His cross is every tree.
              —Author unknown

In every place, in every land
    We can feel the touch of his invisible hand.

I Won't Have to Cross Jordan Alone

We would not be human if we did not fear the unknown. As a child, I was afraid of the dark, because I did not understand the dark. . . . I hated to enter a house about which I knew nothing. . . . As I travel, I do not like to drive over a road that is not marked. Centuries ago—as they do even today—sailors did not like to sail uncharted seas. Ask the average man if he would like to be the first man in space. We just don't like to go to unknown places. Even my first day in school was not too pleasant. It is not strange, then, that we have a tendency to fear death . . . and what's on the other side. No one has ever come back to tell us what it is like on the other side of the Great Divide. But I like to remind myself that because of God, I don't have to face it by myself . . . that I don't have to cross Jordan alone!

If We Never Meet Again

Have you ever stood on the front step of your home and waved good-bye to friends with the realization that you might never see them again? When you left some of your buddies whom you met while in the service, did you have that uneasy feeling inside that told you you would never see them again? That word *never* has a tremendous impact on one's emotions. The young lover leaves and his parting words are, "If we never meet again, I shall always love you!" I could cite many incidents that would stir your emotions, but let me say only that there is one consolation: As we see a loved one depart, we can say with conviction, "If we never meet again on this earth, we know that in that place just beyond the Great Divide, we shall be united!"

I Found the Answer—I Learned to Pray

Many times I have sat in church and other places and listened to prayers. . . . Many times, these prayers seem to be one-sided . . . as though we did not have time to present two sides. . . . How we pray . . . for what we pray . . . the kind of prayer we pray . . . the condition of our heart . . . all are important.

There are two special prayers that we . . . should take the time to say . . in striving for accomplishments . . . to glorify the day . . . a prayer when we are starting out . . . to do a certain deed . . . that we may have the guidance and . . . the courage to succeed . . . and second a prayer of thanks . . . for all the strength and grace . . . with which the Lord enables us . . . to run a worthy race. . . . We may not be triumphant, but . . . we ought to be aware . . . that out of every gain we make . . . the Lord deserves His share . . . and He is just as eager to . . . receive our grateful praise . . . as He is glad to help our hearts . . . to strive for better days.

Many of our problems would be answered if we learned to pray.

I Can Call Jesus Anytime

When troubles come your way, where do you turn? It is not always easy to find someone to help with your problems. You can see your dentist or doctor by appointment. . . . You can see your lawyer by appointment. . . . You can see your banker by appointment. We live in an age of appointments. . . . We have to wait. Sometimes we have to get an appointment to talk to our pastor. But there is a ray of sunshine: It doesn't matter what my problems are . . . how serious or how small. . . . I can call Jesus anytime!

Jesus Fills Our Every Need

Why not follow the trend all the way? We go to the supermarket for all our grocery needs. . . . We go to the bank for all our financial needs. . . . A big department store takes care of many of our other needs. . . . We even go to the big clinics to have our physical being taken care of. Many of us are clamoring for a superbusiness that can take care of all our needs. We want a "one stop" shopping place. But I doubt that we will ever be able to find a place on earth that will take care of our every need. Man is too finite . . . and as he solves some problems, others have a way of bobbing up. I will let you in on a secret—it really isn't a secret, but right here in our midst—all around us is the answer . . . someone who has the capacity to solve all our problems. All we have to do is recognize that Jesus—and Jesus only—fills our every need!

Jesus, I Believe What You Said!

We have just finished months and months of Watergate . . . and we have reached a plateau of life on which we are finding it extremely difficult to believe anything or anyone. The news media come out with accusations, only to have the news the next day contradict the statements. A politician runs for office, and during his campaign he makes all kinds of promises. Once he is elected, he has a terrible loss of memory. In our business dealings, we read guarantees. . . . We hear singers extoll the virtues of the singers' personal lives . . . and when the chips are down, we realize that it is just words. This really is tearing down our civilization. We don't really know whom or what to believe. Nearly 2,000 years ago, Jesus said many sayings . . . made many promises . . . and he kept every one of them. It is comforting to know someone in whom we can believe. I join millions who are sincerely saying, "Jesus, I believe what you said!"

Just A Closer Walk with Thee—
the King and I

A small boy's father had died. . . . When asked what had happened to this father, the boy replied with his child's mind, "Daddy went to walk with Jesus, and they walked and walked and walked, and they never came back." As you walk down life's highway—onto the land beyond the sunset—whom would you like to have walk close to you? I have made my decision. . . . I want to have a closer walk with Jesus. . . . What an impressive and lasting picture—my king and I walking down life's highway. . . . Don't you, too, want to have a closer walk with Jesus?

PART IV

Just a Closer Walk with Thee   53
Just as I Am—though My Sins Be as Scarlet   54
Just as I Am—though My Sins Be as Scarlet   55
Keys to the Kingdom   56
Keys to the Kingdom   57
Known Only to Him   58
Known Only to Him   59
Lord, Please Don't Take My Cross Away   60
Love Is Why   61
Love Is Why   62
Love Is Why   63
Merry Christmas   64
My God Is Real   65
My Greatest Moment   66
Nearer to the Heart of God   67

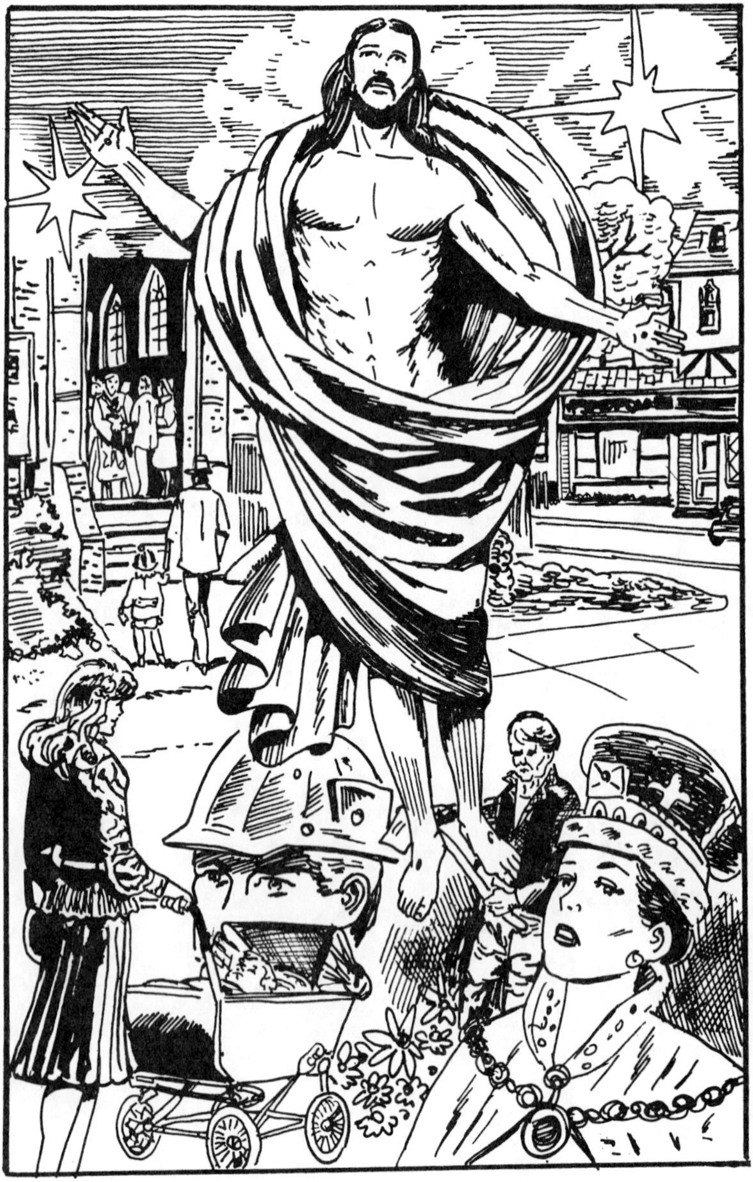

Just a Closer Walk with Thee

Let us do a little thinking this morning. With all of our manifestations of strength and power, we are really weak. There is just one source of real strength and power . . . and there is just one source that can keep us from all harm . . . from all wrong . . . and that can assure our future. Let us face another truth! In all the toils and snares that beset us . . . in all our troubles . . . who really cares? Who can—and will—share our burdens? Who will walk the last mile of the way? And when our time on this earth is over . . . then what? These are thoughts to ponder . . . and to ponder well. I am not a smart person, but I am smart enough to realize that along life's highway I need someone to share my burdens . . . my trials and tribulations. As I approach the twilight of life, I find myself continuously looking to Jesus and saying, "Let me take a closer walk with thee!"

Just as I Am—though My Sins Be as Scarlet

This is Easter! For some it is the time for new dresses . . . new hats . . . new shoes . . . new suits . . . the one-time-of-the-year church attendance. For others, it is the time for renewal of their faith in the future, because it was on this day that Christ arose. He didn't die on the Cross, was buried, and rose again just for the person in a new suit or dress. He died on the Cross for the man in overalls and the woman in gingham dress and apron, as well as for the person who is dressed like a king or queen. He died for the one whose sins are as scarlet and for the one who has experienced salvation. So, on this Easter Day, we can come to Christ for salvation just as we are. Rich or poor . . . young or old . . . saint or sinner, we can come to Him. Though my sins be as scarlet, I can come to Jesus just as I am . . . and so can you!

Just as I Am—though My Sins Be as Scarlet

What kind of cloak are you wearing today? We dress up to go to church. When we are invited out to a formal affair, we have to be sure that we are properly dressed or we will not be welcome—and probably will not be invited again. We have to have certain clothes for certain occasions. We are continuously putting our best foot forward. There is nothing really wrong with that per se. But we are living in an age that does not accept us for what we are, but rather for what we pretend to be. We are wearing a cloak that covers up the real person.

What are you wearing today?

There is something great in the knowledge that God will take us—will welcome us—just as we are, without pretense. All we have to do is place our faith in Him . . . and then we can say to Him, "Just as I am—though my sins be as scarlet—I come to Thee!"

Keys to the Kingdom

Have you ever stopped to think of the many ways we try to get into the kingdom of God? . . . The preachers preach . . . . The teachers teach. . . . The workers work. . . . The leaders lead. . . . We are continuously searching for a way into the kingdom . . . and yet it is so simple—all we need is the keys to the kingdom. . . . As faith unlocks the door, the key unlocks the door. . . . Where is the door? . . . Who has the key? . . . We hold the keys to the kingdom. . . . All we have to do is unlock the door of our hearts and let Jesus in. . . . So simple, isn't it? . . . We hold the keys to the kingdom. . . . Are we going to throw the keys away . . . or will we unlock our hearts and let Jesus come in?

Keys to the Kingdom

Very often we read stories about the key to success, how you can do thus and inherit riches . . . be a wonderful success. How you can by application of certain fundamental rules climb to heights unknown. Keys occupy an important place in our everyday lives. Keys to the cash vault in the bank . . . keys to your car . . . keys to your heart . . . keys that keep you locked into a little world . . . keys that will unlock the doors that lead to riches, fame, fortune. Have you ever stopped to think of the key that you hold that unlocks the door to eternity? Christ is continuously seeking to enter your heart . . . your home . . . your life. He stands at the door of your life, but the lock is on the inside. Only you can unlock it and let Him in. What I am trying to say is that you . . . and you alone . . . hold the keys to the kingdom.

Known Only to Him

Why should we be of so little faith that we spoil our lives worrying about the future?

>Behold
>>The birds
>
>of the Heavens,
>>they sow not,
>
>Neither do they reap,
>>nor gather
>
>into barns,
>>And your Heavenly Father
>
>feedeth them.

>Are not ye
>>of much more
>
>value than they?
>>And which of you,
>
>by being anxious,
>>can add one cubit
>
>unto the measure
>>of your life?

>And why
>>are you anxious
>
>concerning raiments?
>>Consider the lilies
>
>of the field,
>>how they grow.
>
>They toil not,
>>neither do they spin;

> Yet I say unto you
>   that even Solomon
> in all his glory
>   was not arrayed
> like one of these
> —Matthew 6:26–29

I know not what the future holds, but I do know that God and God alone holds the future. What that future holds is a secret known only to Him.

Known Only to Him

Man, through the ages, has sought to look into the future . . . wanted to know what was in the future for him. How many times have you had your fortune told . . . how many times have you wished to know when it was going to rain . . . which way the stock market was going . . . if your sweetheart was going to love you always . . . or how long your job would last? There is nothing unusual about these desires. We all have them. We think we really want to know what God has planned for us while we are here on earth. But did you ever stop to think of what the consequences would be if we really knew? Perhaps it is best that we do not know, but just trust in God. As for me, I know not what the future holds. But I do know that God and God alone holds the future . . . and what the future holds is a secret known only to Him.

Lord, Please Don't Take My Cross Away

America is being tested. Often I have said, and I believe it, that God will never give us a cross without giving us the strength to bear it. Our trials and tribulations . . . our heartaches . . . our reason for tears, burdens and cares . . . our loss of loved ones . . . the way we react to distressing news on radio and TV and in newspapers . . . sickness and death . . . are all means of building character. Remember that fire is the test of gold, but adversity is the test of man. "Too much sun makes a desert." God made man and He knows what it takes to build character and greatness in man. For this reason, I can earnestly say, "Lord, please don't take my cross away!"

Love Is Why

Now is a good time to ask ourselves some questions. Why are we so anxious to play Santa Claus? Why do we like to do things for them . . . our loved ones? Do you look out into space and wonder why God gave us all those beautiful things? Do you wonder why we have life . . . why we are free . . . why God has given us riches untold, or why He will reach down and lift us up from a world of sin? Have you thought why a mother will give her life for her child? Do you wonder why parents will sacrifice so many things for their children? Have you asked yourself why God tolerates our sins and remains patient with us? Why does He ease the pain in our breast when burdens weigh us down? And why does He stand by us when we forget to pray . . . to worship in His sanctuary . . . to give to His cause . . . or to thank Him for bountiful gifts and mercy? Have you asked yourself why He gave us His only begotten Son that we might have eternal life? There is but one answer: Love is why!

Love Is Why

Tell me why a person will reach down and help a crippled child . . . why a mother will sacrifice her life for a child . . . why God gave His only begotten Son? The answer is: *Love is why!*

    A mother said to her adopted child:

    "Not flesh of my flesh,
    Nor bone of my bone,
    But still miraculously
    You are my own.

    "Never forget,
    For a single minute,
    You didn't grow under
    my heart
    But in it!"

When you feel compassion in your heart . . . when you see it in others . . . be still and know that love is why!

Love Is Why

It was love that built the mountains and made the sea. It was love that put beauty into the world. It was love that gave us flowers . . . the rain . . . the sun. It is love that gives us friendships . . . and plants happiness wherever hearts are found. It is love that takes away our suffering and plants within our hearts sweet peace. When we wonder why God has done these marvelous things for us . . . why He gave His only begotten Son . . . we know that love is why!

Merry Christmas

When little children, from two to ninety-two, stand staring through plate glass windows at electric trains chugging through cardboard tunnels, you know it's Christmas. . . . When little children go out in the kitchen and do the dishes—without even being asked—you know it's Christmas. . . . When parents begin dashing from one store to another, clutching a long list in one hand, and go home on the bus where passengers are outnumbered by the packages, you know it's Christmas. . . . When the postman appears at the door bent double by the pack on his back, you know it's Christmas. . . . When parents begin looking more worried than usual and muttering about "cutting down this year," you know it's Christmas. . . . And when all of us open up our hearts and pocketbooks and remember the many people in need at this Christmas season, then all the homeless and hungry and lonely and unfortunate people in our town will know it's Christmas and, thanks to you and your generous heart, a very merry Christmas.

My God Is Real

Read your paper . . . listen to the radio . . . watch television . . . and you will read or hear someone trying to tear down the Kingdom of God. Those people say that God is not real . . . that Jesus is not real . . . that He is just a myth created by some writers long, long ago. Whenever I see a twinkling star . . . or see the rising sun . . . or feel the warmth of summer or chill of winter . . . or see a flower or bird and feel a raindrop . . . or breathe fresh, unseen air into my lungs . . . or hear the cry of a newborn baby . . . these and a million other marvelous things make me know beyond any doubt that my God is real . . . and He's real for you!

My Greatest Moment

What has been your greatest moment in life? When you pulled some smart business deal . . . when you were elected to some high office . . . when you were acclaimed by the crowd as an outstanding person . . . when you were married . . . when your first child was born? My greatest moment came one Wednesday morning when I was fifteen. I slipped away from my work and went down to a Methodist church where a revival was being held. In the quiet of that early morning, God reached down and put His hand in mine and lifted me up. It was then and there I accepted Jesus as my personal savior. That was . . . still is . . . and will always be . . . my greatest moment. What you consider your greatest moment determines which way you shall go in life and death.

Near to the Heart of God

A day never passes that doesn't include a desire on our part to be associated with the better things in life. Whether or not we do anything about it is another matter. We want to be in the hearts of our wives . . . our sweethearts . . . our children or parents. We like to be in the thoughts of those who mean much to us. We aspire to be near and to be included in the plans of those dearest to us. I am thinking of how important it is to concentrate on being close to that which makes the greatest contribution to our way of life . . . to our eternity. Why not pattern our lives so that whatever we do . . . whatever we say . . . whatever we even think . . . will help us to be near to the heart of God?

PART V

No Greater Love   71
No One Stands Alone   72
Nothing Can Compare   73
Not My Will   74
Not My Will   75
Not My Will   76
Not My Will   77
One by One   78
Put Your Hand in the Hand of the Man from Galilee   79
Reach Out for Jesus   80
Remind Me, Dear Lord!   81
Riding the Range with Jesus   82
Room at the Cross   83
Searching for You   84
Shall I Crucify My Savior?   85

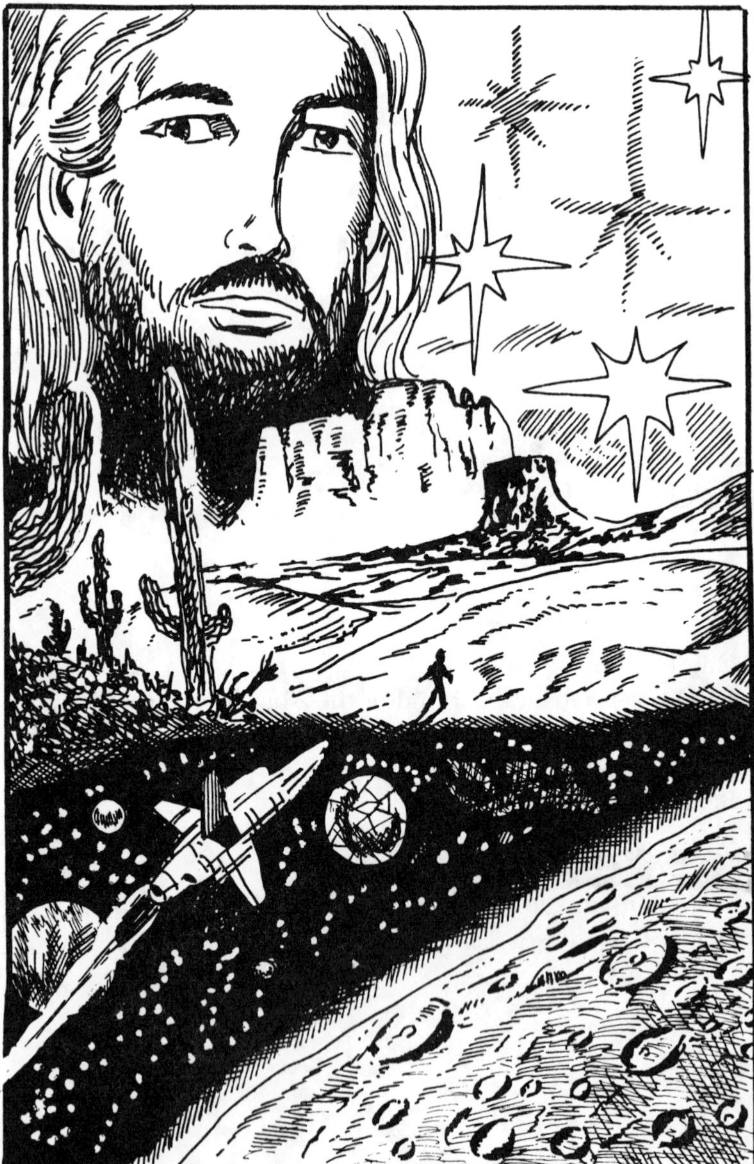

No Greater Love

Love is defined as a strong and deep feeling of attachment . . . great affection. "Greater love hath no man than to lay down his life for a friend." Love rules the world. Without love, the world would perish. The love of a man for a maid . . . the love of a mother for a child . . . the love of a child for a parent . . . the love that dominates and motivates young lovers . . . the deep and abiding love of a husband and wife, which endures through the years . . . yes, love controls the universe . . . the human emotions. Without love, life would be void and empty. But there is *no greater love* . . . anywhere . . . anytime than the love of God.

No One Stands Alone

I know that you have seen pictures of a person standing in the middle of a desert, surrounded by nothing but space. Perhaps you have had that experience. . . . You probably have seen pictures of a spaceship out in that void that surrounds the earth. When you were a child—and probably since you grew up—you have had the feeling that you were all alone . . . that no one cared . . . that you had to face the future alone. That is not such a pleasant feeling. It is good to know that in the land of God, no one stands alone. He is always beside you.

Nothing Can Compare

It is difficult these days to watch TV without having to watch numerous commericals comparing certain products with others. Compare this cigarette with any other cigarette and taste the difference . . . take this tablet and see how much faster you get relief . . . compare this car with others in the low-priced field . . . use this type of cleaner and see the difference. But nothing will give you faster relief from a world of care than Jesus . . . nothing will taste better than Christian living . . . nothing will wash you cleaner and make you whiter than the blood of Jesus. When you start selling the Gospel to this world, there's nothing that can compare!

Not My Will

In the poem "The Charge of the Light Brigade" is a line "Theirs, not mine to reason why, theirs but to do or die." The soldier is told to obey his superior without question. As children, we used to depend on our fathers and mothers for guidance. We never questioned their judgment. But as we grew older, we began to think for ourselves and to make decisions on our own. They were not always right and today our decisions are not always right. But God gives us a choice. We can choose which way we shall go. We are free agents. We can be selfish or we can be generous . . . we can be harsh or we can be kind . . . we can love or we can hate . . . we can save or we can kill . . . we can take God into our lives or we can shut him out. What decision are we going to make? Are we willing to surrender to His will? Or shall we depend on our limited and finite minds to lead us into our future? Jesus prayed, "Not my will, but Thine be done." And please, God, may this same prayer be mine every day.

Not My Will

We can make all kinds resolutions for the New Year. . . . In fact, we do make all kinds. And few are those that we keep. So, instead of making a long list of things we shall resolve to do or not to do, let us make just one big resolution and then concentrate on that one and keep it! Let's have a little talk with God and say to him, "This year it shall be Thy will, not mine!"

Not My Will

The following prayer could very well be the greatest prayer that we could ever make:

> I lay me down
> > In peace and sleep.
>
> I pray Thee, God,
> > My soul to keep.
>
> And as I rest,
> > This prayer I make:
>
> To do Thy will
> > When I awake.

Not My Will

Suppose we were continuously asking for things we should not ask for. . . . Suppose each time we knelt to pray, we found ourselves praying for things selfishly. . . . Suppose our lives were centered around asking for ourselves instead of asking a few things for our neighbors. . . . That would indicate that our hearts are hard and selfish . . . our minds dull and narrow . . . our eyes dimmed by greed. It would indicate that we need to throw off our robe of flesh, which is making us falter. Let us pray, "Not my will, but Thine be done." That is how Jesus prayed. Why can't we have the same prayer in our hearts, too? He will guide our steps. . . . He will hold our hands. Let us pray earnestly and sincerely, "Not my will, but Thine be done!"

One by One

When you were young and started marching down life's highway, there were many people marching with you. . . . As the years have come and gone, many of those friends and loved ones have dropped out . . . one by one. . . . You ask yourself, "Who will be next? . . . Will I be next? . . . Where did they go? . . . Where will I go?" Be not concerned—just open up your heart and let Jesus in . . . and then when that time comes for you to be another to drop out of the marching column . . . He will lead you safely home . . . to dwell among the immortals.

Put Your Hand in the Hand of the Man from Galilee

As children we felt secure when we could put our hand in the hand of our mother. . . . What a wonderful feeling when young lovers hold hands as they walk down lovers' lane . . . (not a bad idea for some of us old people). . . . What a thrill when you grasp the hand of an old friend. . . . It is so reassuring when you are in deep trouble to have someone take your hand and place their arm around your shoulder. . . . But when the chips are really down and you are wallowing in the Slough of Despondency . . . when you feel that everything and everyone are against you . . . when you are saying, "Oh, what's the use?" . . . let me make a suggestion that will take you safely across that bridge of despair: Just put your hand in the hand of the man from Galilee!

Reach Out for Jesus

We are living in a complex world . . . full of strife, anxiety, confusion! . . . We seem to have no sense of direction. We are constantly reaching out for a solution to our problems . . . dilemmas. We turn to drugs, alcohol . . . immoral living . . . demonstrations . . . protests . . . rebellion. We want a change without knowing what or why. We try to blame it all on someone else. We think our government . . . the Supreme Court . . . United Nations . . . our congressman or president can furnish the solution to our misdirected lives. Some of us even think money is the solution. It does help in some matters. Yet the solution is simple, so very simple. It is amazing . . . fantastic . . . that a nation that is so well educated, so seemingly brilliant . . . so blessed with leadership qualities that we think we can solve the whole world's problems yet can't recognize the simple solution. We have only to reach out for Jesus!

Remind Me, Dear Lord!

Most of us are reluctant to have someone remind us of something we have forgotten . . . or something we promised to do but didn't. In business, we call it efficiency expertise. . . . In marriage, we call it nagging. We resent our parents . . . minister . . . associates reminding us of our responsibilities . . . obligations . . . wrongdoing. But God laid down some fundamental rules and regulations with which we must comply if we are to inheit eternal life or even get the maximum benefit out of our earthly home. Each morning as I begin a new day, I whisper a prayer and say, "Remind me, dear Lord!"

Riding the Range with Jesus

If we were to preface everything by asking ourselves, "What would Jesus do?" or "What would Jesus think?" we certainly wouldn't get into much trouble, would we? . . . Just to see how we get along next week, let's take him with us while we work . . . while we play golf . . . or go fishing . . . or play bridge . . . let him help us whenever we sell something . . . or make a business deal . . . take him riding with us . . . let him listen to our conversation. . . . Another way of expressing what I am trying to suggest is . . . let's ride the range with Jesus.

Room at the Cross

There are a lot of big things in the world, the Grand Canyon . . . New York City . . . the Pacific Ocean . . . not to mention the national debt. In spite of this bigness, there is concern that within a few years our exploding population will be crying for more room. Today, in many cities, there is a congestion that is stifling . . . that is breeding crime and poverty. Our highways are jammed . . . our parking places are at a premium. And I guess that in time air travel will be filled with collisions because of the heavy traffic. But there is one consolation: In God's Kingdom there is room and there will be room. Not because of the few people there, but because of the bigness of God's heart. His heart is big enough for all. At the Cross on which Jesus died is a place for you and me. In spite of how crowded we may feel . . . how closed in . . . it is good to know that there is room at the Cross.

Searching for You

Some years ago, I read a book titled *The Search*. As I remember that book, I think of some of the searching that is going on daily:

> A worldly man searching for fame and fortune
> A woman searching for a husband (that is, a person to be her husband)
> A student searching for knowledge
> A family man searching for money to pay his bills
> A preacher searching for the Scriptures
> A society woman searching for higher social position
> A scientist searching for the secret of life
> An astronomer searching for undiscovered planets

The list could go on and on . . . and all the time Jesus is searching for you and me. . . . He is searching for the man or woman . . . boy or girl . . . who is ready to take up his cross and follow wherever he leads them. Let us sincerely . . . earnestly . . . prayerfully . . . say, "Here I am, Lord. Search for me no longer."

Shall I Crucify My Savior?

His enemies took Jesus out to a hill and crucified him by nailing him to a cross. That was over 1,900 years ago. Today we are still crucifying him. We don't have to drive nails into his hands and feet and hang him on a cross to crucify him.

By our actions . . . by our thoughts . . . by our deeds . . . we crucify him. By our sins of commission . . . by our sins of omission . . . we crucify him. Every time we speak an unkind word . . . gossip about our neighbors . . . do an unkind act . . . we crucify him. Every time we neglect to help a less fortunate brother or sister . . . use profane or obscene language . . . we crucify him. Every time we purposely don't go to his house of worship . . . give to his kingdom . . . fail to witness for him . . . criticize others . . . we crucify him. Every time we cheat . . . or lie . . . we crucify him. Every time we let our position . . . our clout . . . our money make us vain . . . ruthless . . . we crucify him. When we become unkind . . . selfish . . . arrogant . . . self-centered . . . we crucify him. When we are selfishly inconsiderate of others . . . fail to read his Holy Word . . . neglect to pray . . . practice infidelity . . . have evil thoughts . . . we crucify him.

When you are tempted to talk about your neighbor . . . do an unkind deed . . . make excuses for not doing your duty to your fellow citizens . . . your family . . . your church . . . ask youself, "Shall I crucify him?" As we observe the Resurrection of Jesus this Easter, let us search our hearts and ask ourselves over and over, "Shall I crucify him?"

What are we doing today? Crucifying him or exalting his name . . . displaying homage to the devil or putting this evil one behind us?

What shall we do today? Crucify him or exalt him?

PART VI

Stranger from Galilee   89
Sweet Hour of Prayer   90
Take My Hand, Precious Lord—Invisible Hands—
    Blessed Jesus, Hold My Hands   91
Take My Hand, Precious Lord   92
Take Time to Be Holy   93
Taller than Trees   94
The Cross Made the Difference   95
The Gentle Stranger   96
The Joy of Knowing Jesus   97
The King and I   98
The Love of God   99
The Old Rugged Cross   100
The Old Rugged Cross   101

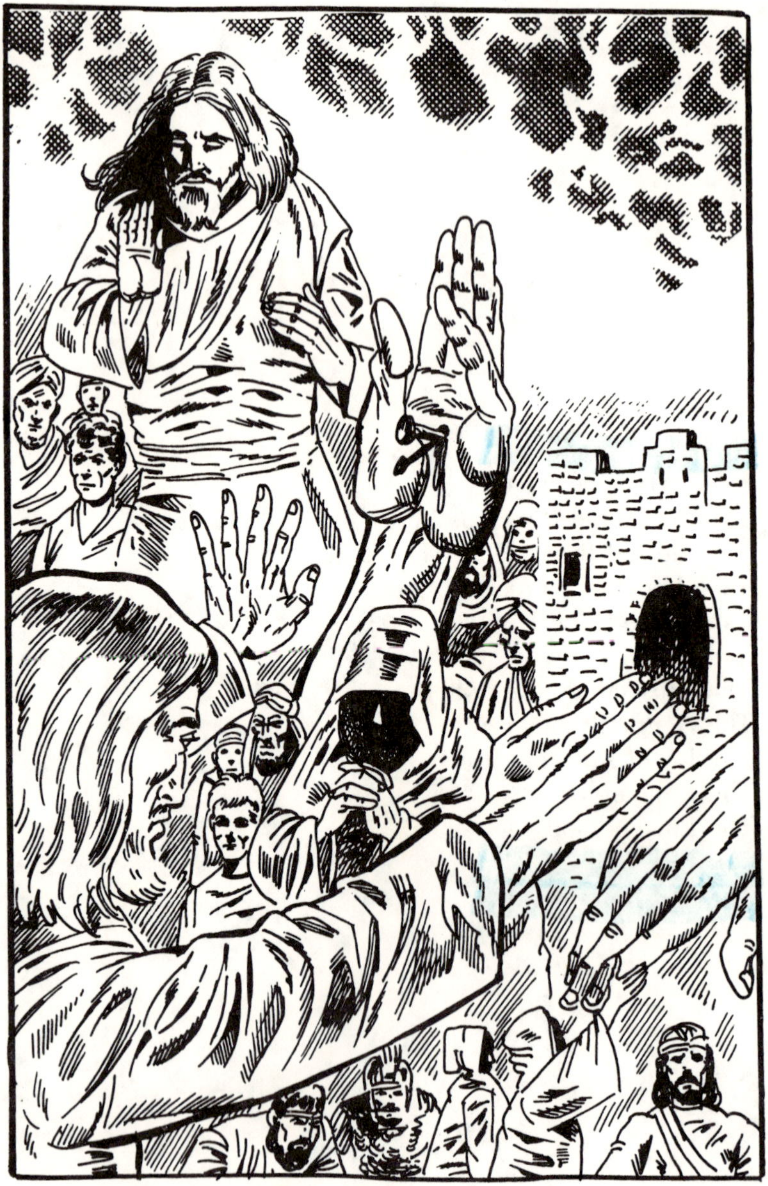

Stranger from Galilee

One of the most tragic events of history is that Jesus walked by the Sea of Galilee and to thousands who saw him he was a stranger. Today he is still a stranger to millions. What if those people two thousand years ago had recognized and accepted Jesus as a friend . . . a companion . . . a savior? Billions upon billions of tears through the centuries would never have been shed. God's greatest gift to man—His only begotten Son, a man who should be in the hearts and lives of everyone—to millions of people he is still the stranger from Galilee. How about you? Do you know Jesus? Do you realize what a friend you have in Jesus? Is Jesus all the world to you . . . or is He still the stranger from Galilee?

Sweet Hour of Prayer

What time of day is the most meaningful to you? Is it at the break of dawn, when the sun is showering the world with the brightness of a new day? Is it at noon, when you pause in the midst of the throng? Or is it when twilight shadows lengthen to close another day . . . and you journey home to family and the comforts of home and fireside? Perhaps it is when you close your eyes and fall asleep, to shut out the sorrows and disappointments of a busy day.

Or could the sweetest—the most comforting—the most meaningful—time be the sweet hour of prayer that calls you from a world of care? When my world is tumbling down and my burdens too much to bear, I find refuge in a sweet hour of prayer with my Heavenly Father.

If you would have an unforgettable experience, why don't you, too, take time out from a busy and hectic world for a sweet hour of prayer?

What a difference it will make!

Take My Hand, Precious Lord—
Invisible Hands—
Blessed Jesus, Hold My Hands

Many times on our program we have emphasized the importance of hands . . . the hand of God . . . the invisible hands that guide us through life and eternity. . . . He reached out and touched the blind man and caused him to see. . . . He stretched forth his hand, and a man took up his bed and walked. . . . Someone reached forth a hand and touched the hem of his garment and was made whole. . . . His hands grasped the handle of the whip, and he drove the money changers out of the temple. . . . With his hands, he gave the woman at the well a cup of water. . . . His hands were placed beneath his chin as he prayed in the Garden of Gethsemane. . . . His hands pointed to the sins of the world, and it was those hands that were nailed to the Cross. . . . And those same hands can lift a world from the depths of sin onto a throne in Heaven. . . . Take my hand, precious Lord, and place it in Thy invisible Hands and hold me close to Thee.

Take My Hand, Precious Lord

"Daddy, take my hand!" is a familiar request. When you walk down the street in the night, you can feel the tug of a little hand in yours as your child seeks the protection of an earthly father. Have you ever knelt at the bedside of a close friend or loved one and had them reach for you and say, "Bill, hold my hand"? Have you ever sat in church—or at the movies—and had your boyfriend or girl friend reach out and touch your hand? And isn't it a wonderful feeling to meet an old friend and clasp his hand in renewal of a true friendship!

> Remember that your smile
> Lights up the world awhile,
> That others feel cast down
> Because they see your frown,
> And just your friendly touch
> Can often mean so much!

And it does! And so does the touch of God's hand in mine. It is not strange or unusual that I often say, "Take my hand, precious Lord."

Take Time to Be Holy

A few days ago, we were busy getting ready to celebrate Thanksgiving . . . although we do sometimes have a peculiar way of celebrating it. And now comes the excitement of getting ready for Christmas, although often it does not mean getting ready for Christ. So many things to do . . . so many places to go . . . so many things to buy. When you ask someone to do something for someone else, you often get the reply, "I don't have time; there is so much to do." In the morning, it is the usual rush to get to the office for the coffee break . . . get the kids off to school or make preparations for the bridge party. At noon, we rarely take time out for lunch—at least a leisurely lunch. . . . At night, we rush home to get ready to go somewhere or to do something we consider really important. . . . Sometimes our children ask, "Where's Daddy?" or "Where's Mommie?" And we don't have time to make friends with the man on the street. Even when we go to church, we are concerned about the length of the sermon . . . the prayers . . . the service. Yes, we are living in a day of hurly-burly . . . not really taking time out to live. Don't you agree that it behoves us to pause at the break of day . . . in the midst of the throng . . . or at twilight . . . somewhere . . . somehow . . . sometime . . . and take time to be holy!

Taller than Trees

Have you ever noticed what happens when you stand close to a light? Notice how tall your shadow is . . . and when you stand far away your shadow is smaller? You can measure your life by the length of the shadow you cast. The closer you stand to Jesus, the taller your shadow will be. . . . The farther away from Jesus you stand, the smaller your shadow will be. Begin today—right now—to stand close to God and grow tall—taller than trees.

The Cross Made the Difference

The man was beset with sin . . . resorted to drugs . . . immoral living . . . was unscrupulous in his business affairs . . . a real "hell on wheels" with no principles . . . the type of person you really had no respect for! Then he suddenly blossomed forth like a ray of sunshine right out of Heaven's blue. His frown replaced with a smile . . . cruelty with kindness . . . greed with unselfishness . . . intolerance with understanding . . . hatred with love . . . a new man had emerged! Being human, we ask, "What happened? Why the difference?" We were overwhelmed with joy when we recognized that the old rugged Cross made the difference!

The Gentle Stranger

To many people two thousand years ago Jesus was just a gentle stranger . . . kind and considerate, but nothing more. What is he to you? If we were walking down the street and met the Master face to face, would you recognize him for what he is? . . . Or would you be too busy with your worldly thoughts and plans to have a heart and mind that would see and know him—not just a gentle stranger, but our everlasting friend and savior? When we look into the world through a clear window, we can see the beauties God intended for us to see, but when we cover the glass with silver, we make it a mirror and see only ourselves. Do not let the material things of life blot out our view of the gentle stranger . . . a person who should be recognized and known to all of us as God's greatest gift to mankind.

The Joy of Knowing Jesus

There are many things that bring joy into our lives! The joy of a newfound love . . . your boss has just promoted you and given you a raise in salary . . . your first baby has been born, and mother and child are doing well . . . your sweetheart has accepted your marriage proposal and said, "I'll always love you!" . . . your team has just won the homecoming game! . . . the joy of freedom! . . . and hundreds of other joyful moments! . . . But these are really only temporary! However, there is a joy that transcends all others and lasts forever! It is the joy of knowing Jesus!

The King and I

We may worship silver and gold. . . . We may pay homage to the things of the flesh. . . . We may fall postrate at the foot of our passion. . . . We may bow down to fame and fortune and popularity. . . . We may burn incense at the altar of greed and hatred. . . . But there is only one king—only one personality—to whom we should go on bended knees . . . only one person to whom we should swear allegiance . . . and that is God! . . . And he was a stranger to me—a foreigner—until one day He placed his arm around me . . . and now—thanks to the greatness of His heart—the King and I walk hand in hand down life's highway. . . . Won't you join us?

The Love of God

The love of God knows no bounds. It reaches from east to west . . . from north to south . . . far and wide . . . from the highest star to the lowest Hell. No pen or tongue can ever describe the infinite love of God. So when we say or sing:

> Should auld acquaintance be forgot
> And never brought to mind.
> Then drink a cup of kindness, dear,
> For Auld Lang Syne.

Let us not forget the most important thing to remember . . . and that is the love of God—the love that will lead us safely through the next year.

The Old Rugged Cross

There would be no Easter had there been no rugged cross. . . . There would be no tomorrow if there had been no Resurrection. . . . There would be no Resurrection if God had not promised to redeem all men and give them eternal life. As cruel as Christ's death on the Cross was, it was necessary if we are to inherit eternal life. That cross is the emblem of suffering and shame. But Jesus went to that cross for you and me. Jesus was crucified on that cross because he loves us. Let us not continue to keep him on that cross by the sinful lives we lead. The least we can do on this Resurrection Morning is to be loyal to that old rugged cross . . . which we can someday exchange for a crown!

The Old Rugged Cross

Christmas will soon be here. After that will come the days when we begin exchanging our Christmas gifts for something else . . . at least for a different size. But there is another exchange we can make that will last throughout eternity. Many, many times we have sung the immortal song, "The Old Rugged Cross." Some of us sing it with full meaning. . . . Others just sing it without thought or feeling. There are those who see the old rugged cross standing on a faraway hill, emblematic of suffering and shame. Others see a wondrous beauty as they realize that it was on that cross that Jesus suffered and died for them . . . and for us. So we cherish the old rugged cross—our cross—and someday we will exchange that cross for a crown. "For God so loved the world that He gave His only begotten Son!" What a challenging thought we should have in our hearts and minds as we listen to "The Old Rugged Cross"!

PART VII

When They Ring Those Golden Bells   105
When They Ring Those Golden Bells   105
We Can Call Jesus Anytime   106
What a Day That Will Be   107
What a Day That Will Be   108
What a Friend I Have in Jesus   109
What Would I Do without Jesus?   110
When He Reached Down His Hand   111
When He Reached Down His Hand   112
When I Met the Master   113
Where No One Stands Alone   114
Where No One Stands Alone—What a Day That Will Be   114
The Old Rugged Cross   115
Wherever He Leads Me I Will Follow   116
Whispering Hope   117

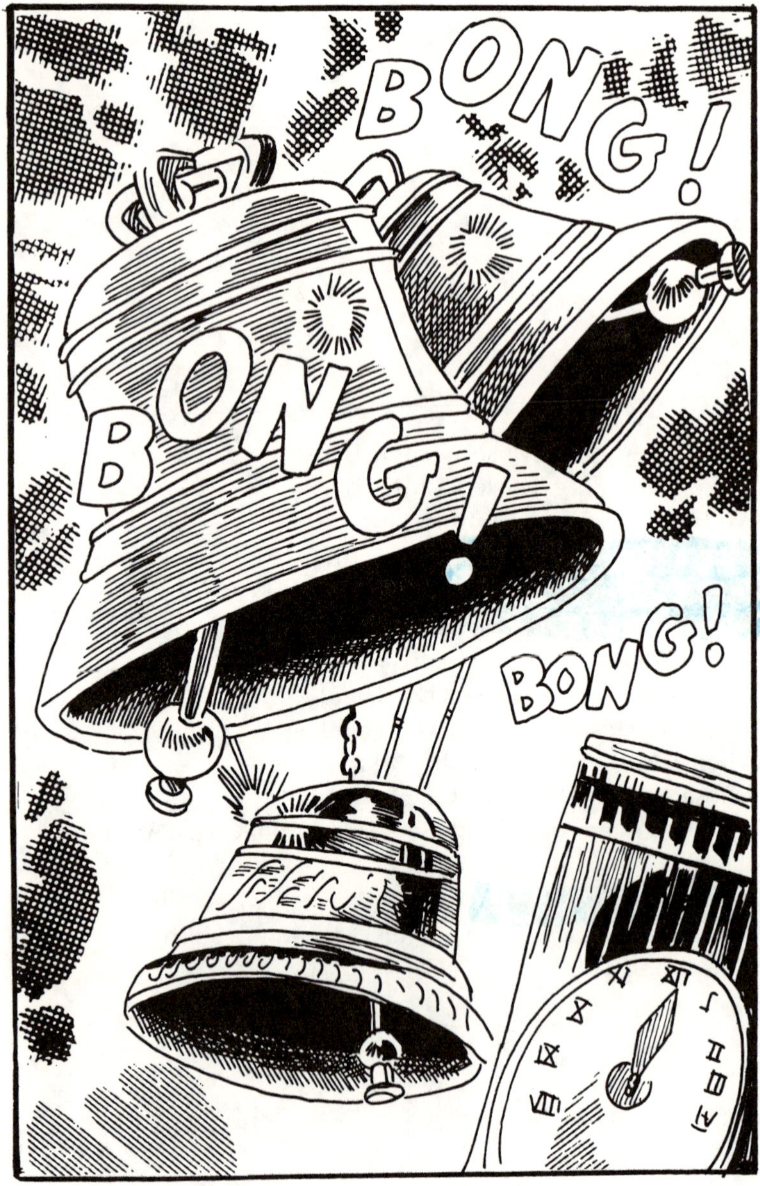
BONG!
BONG!
BONG!

When They Ring Those Golden Bells

Last night, people all over the world rang out the old year and rang in the new. At midnight, the bells were ringing and people were singing. Bells were the order of the day—or, rather, the night. They rang a toast for old friends . . . for new acquaintances. They rang them for you and for me. It was exciting . . . thrilling . . . a wonderful experience . . . but somehow as I enter the new year, I can't help but think of another time when we shall rejoice at the sound of bells, and that is when they ring those golden bells for you and me. What a day that will be.

When They Ring Those Golden Bells

Did you ever live on a farm in those days when they had dinner bells and from across the fields about noontime would come the welcome sound of the bell . . . the call to dinner? It was dinner in those days, not lunch. Did you ever hear the sound of a cowbell drifting across the meadows? There has always been something inspiring about mission bells. And what sweeter sound can there be than the church bell of the old country church where we spent our childhood . . . the tolling of the bell that told that it was time for us to go to church to worship in God's sanctuary? But there will be another time when we shall rejoice at the sound of bells . . . and that is when they ring those golden bells for you and me!

We Can Call Jesus Anytime

The doctor doesn't like for you to call him after office hours unless it is absolutely necessary. . . . The bank often closes at 1 o'clock, and your banker doesn't like to be bothered after that. . . . Your lawyer would rather have you make an appointment . . . and I haven't checked with my pastor lately, but it is probable that an appointment with him would be in order. . . . Many times we hesitate to call our closest friend except at certain times . . . and you mustn't dare call a person while his favorite TV show is on. . . . I guess we live in a more-or-less appointment age. . . . But we do have a person who is our friend, our doctor, our physician, our teacher. He is our pastor . . . he is our treasure house of real values . . . and he is pleading our case. . . . That person is Jesus . . . and isn't it wonderful that we can call Jesus anytime?

What a Day That Will Be

What a day that will be. What day? The day you get married? The day you get that job or raise? Perhaps it's the day you start your vacation or the day your first child is born. Or maybe it's Christmas Day. We all have a day we look forward to . . . and that day varies with each of us. What is important to one person may not be important to another. It may be the day you make your last payment on your car or wedding ring! But there is a day that should concern all of us . . . and that is the day we meet the Master face to face . . . that day when we shall sit on the Throne of Grace . . . that day when all the cares of this world vanish and we enter into a place of eternal joy and peace! In the rush of everyday living, it is sometimes difficult to visualize that day beyond the Great Divide. But when we stop to think . . . when we begin to look beyond the sunset and appreciate what is in store for us if we walk in the footsteps of our Master . . . I think we, too, will say with feeling and enthusiasm, "What a day that will be!"

What a Day That Will Be

The thing that makes life interesting is anticipation. When we were children, in our world the last part of the year centered around the prospect of seeing Santa Claus or at least finding out what he was going to leave for us. We look forward to the football game . . . our first date . . . our wedding . . . a child in the home . . . seeing Mom and Dad. And for Christians the occasion will be when we meet the Master face to face. . . . What a day that will be.

What a Friend I Have in Jesus

The Scriptures say: "Where your treasure is there will be your heart also." My greatest treasure is my friend . . . who always is the same . . . in poverty or plenty and in humbleness or fame . . . who comforts me when skies are gray . . . and . . . everything goes wrong . . . and counsels me to try again . . . with courage new and strong. . . . He is the one whose kindly words . . . so much inspire me . . . to live a better life each day . . . and practice charity. . . . In every way He shows that He . . . is generous and true . . . any favor I may ask . . . He is prepared to do. . . . And someday I may search the world . . . for riches I have known. . . . But I shall never be without . . . this friend I call my own. . . . It is with complete sincerity that I say, "What a friend I have in Jesus."

What Would I Do without Jesus?

The most important question today is, what would I do without Jesus? If you're keeping abreast of current events, you will realize that there is a worldwide movement on foot to blot the name of Jesus from the world. No reference is to be made to Jesus in literature . . . on TV . . . or radio . . . in newspapers . . . or in motion pictures. Recently a suit was filed in federal court asking that the name of Jesus be omitted from public schools . . . that the Bible be removed from public libraries . . . that no classroom discussion or assignments include the name of Jesus. This is an insidious movement and one of which I can only say, "America, wake up!"

When He Reached Down His Hand

We are living in an age of space and speed . . . faster cars to get someplace quicker . . . faster planes to take more people to more places in less time. . . . The Soviet Union and the United States are struggling to be the first to get men onto distant planets. . . . We are trying frantically to conquer space. . . . The Soviets think they have really done something by getting tons of metal, et cetera, several thousands of miles into the vast void beyond the earth's surface. . . . So do the Americans. . . . But what about God? . . . Who can reach down and take a person from the depths of hell . . . and in the twinkling of an eye transplant him onto a place on a throne in Heaven? . . . That is something that conquers time, space, and distance. . . . We should be so thankful that because of His love He can—and does—reach down his hand for you and me and places us in eternal peace and joy.

When He Reached Down His Hand

Every day we see people who delight in knocking the fellow who is already down, with never a thought of reaching down and lending a helping hand. "No man stands so tall as he who stoops to help a crippled child!" That can be said of anyone who stoops to help a less fortunate brother. Do you feel that you are too good to help someone in need? Do you sometimes say no when asked to help in a worthy cause? Do you reply, "I don't have that in my budget," or "My budget is already spent"? When you need the help of God desperately, how would you feel if He should say, "No, my passion for you is already spent. You will have to come back next year"? It is good to know that God does not feel that He is too good . . . too busy . . . to reach down and pick us up from whatever gutter we have fallen into. I think—and I think with deep appreciation—when I hear the song "When He Reached Down His Hand!"

How about you?

When I Met the Master

Have you ever realized that the decisions we are making today are determing the type of people we will be tomorrow? When we come face to face with a problem, the decision we make to solve that problem will affect our entire life. We are daily cutting the pattern of our lives. Our daily decisions make some kind of contribution to our future. We cannot turn back the pages of time. What will happen when we meet the Master face to face? What will we do? . . . what will we say? . . . How will we act? . . . Whatever our decision, our eternity will be affected. Let us make the decision now to pray that when we do meet the Master face to face, we will have the wisdom to make the right decision.

Where No One Stands Alone

Have you ever had that "all alone" feeling? Do you remember when you refused to follow the crowd . . . when you did not participate in certain activities while everyone else was doing those things? Have you ever been considered "off limits" to a certain type of boy or girl because you did not bow to the demands of that particular type of boy or girl or his or her fast set? Have you ever stood for a principle—whether it be political . . . partisan . . . or sectarian—when the crowd was running wild in the opposite direction? If you have . . . then you know how it feels to stand alone. But as long as you stand for the right things in life, you are not standing alone! There is always someone beside you. As long as you are on God's side, you are where no one stands alone!

Where No One Stands Alone— What a Day That Will Be

Through the ages, man has had to stand alone—away from the crowd. Statesmen who fought alone for the best interests of their country . . . . Christians who have had to stand alone as they faced their persecutors . . . boys and girls who have had to stand alone because of their high principles. A pastor sometimes has to stand alone before his congregation. I could go on and on, but there will come a day when no one stand alone . . . and what a day that will be.

The Old Rugged Cross

The Cross is such a simple thing. Yet men have talked and sung about it through the ages. It is a ladder to the skies . . . a signboard on the road . . . and a key that fits the door to joys untold. It is a signal to the human race that God is merciful. To some, it is a stumbling block, but to others it is a stepping-stone to grace. The Cross is an anchor in the storm . . . a hammer against oppression and a sword to fight the battles of the Lord. . . . It is more than a tree on the hill; it is a window for the soul. . . . The Cross is a simple thing, but it shines forth into the world because of the One identified with it, Jesus.

Wherever He Leads Me I Will Follow

It is interesting how by habit we drift into certain patterns. . . . We have certain times to do specific things. . . . For instance—we worship on Sunday. . . . It never occurs us that worship should be a daily—hourly—experience instead of a weekly one. . . . Prayer should be at any time of the day or night—not just on Sunday. . . . I was just thinking of what would happen if God had only certain times when He would look after us . . . administer to our needs . . . have compassion on us . . . but he is a little more generous . . . and just as he is ready to serve and help us day or night—twenty-four hours, I think we should be willing to follow wherever He leads us—not for just a minute, not for just an hour, not for just a year . . . but twenty-four hours each day—for always. . . . Night or day, wherever He leads me I will follow. . . .

Whispering Hope

Something to do
Something to love
Something to hope for

For many years, that has been my theme to live by. Without these three things, my life is not complete. And certainly life without hope is void . . . meaningless. We hope the sun will shine tomorrow . . . the stars will twinkle tonight . . . we will get that raise we planned for . . . our business will be successful . . . we will win that golf match tomorrow . . . our team will win . . . our marriage proposal will be accepted . . . and on and on and on. Right now, I am hoping that Santa Claus will come to see me. And I hope that everyone this Christmas will have the merriest one they ever had. And I not only hope, but pray, that it will be a safe Christmas and that the true spirit of Christmas will reign supreme! A song that has always found a responsive chord in my heart, and one that has been an inspiration through the years, is the ever popular . . . inspiring . . . challenging . . . promising "Whispering Hope."

PART VIII

White Christmas 121
With His Hand in Mine! 122
Crowded World 123
I Depend on Him 124
Teach Me, Lord 125
The Handicapped and God 126
Walking with God 127

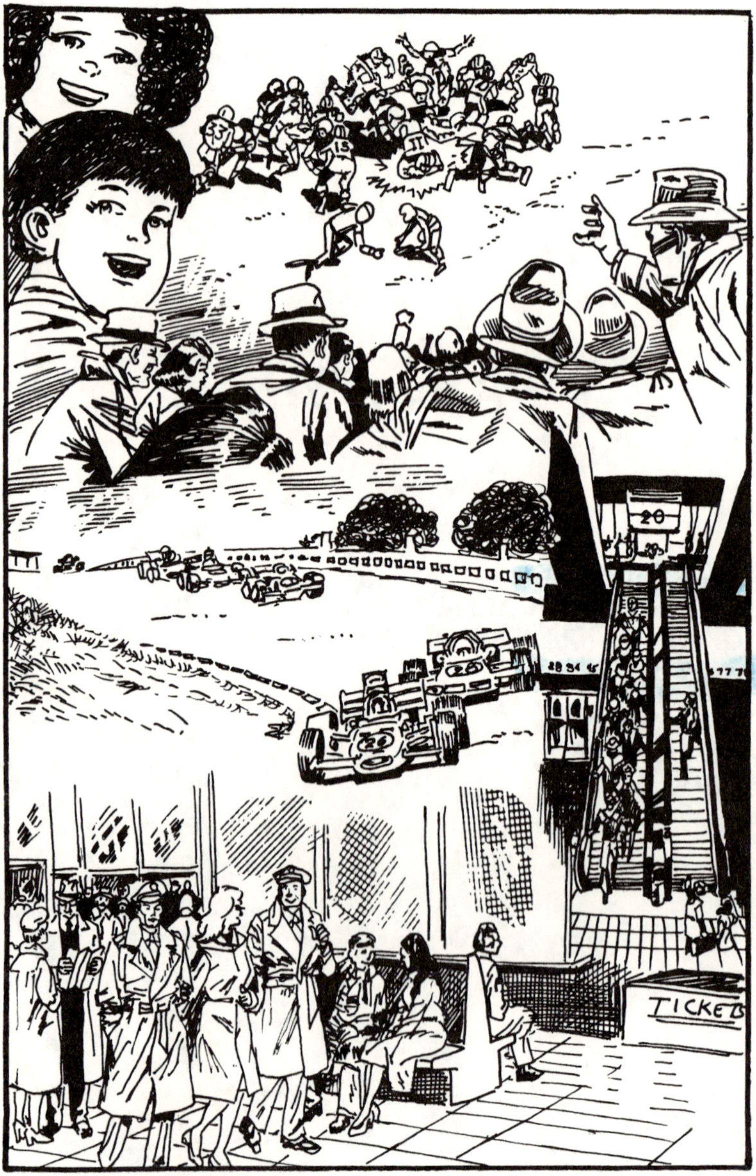
20

White Christmas

Are you dreaming of a white Christmas? . . . let me tell you a secret . . . and it all concerns who is in your home today—Christmas Day:

How many hours in your home will Jesus be your welcome
 guest?
And will you treat him as well or better than the rest?
You need not serve him food and drink or entertain him
 there,
But only remember Him, with now and then a prayer.
To show him that you love Him, by the way you love each
 other—
Your wife, your husband, mother, dad, sister or brother.
Your virtues are his dinner, and your prayer becomes his
 drink.
And you can keep him happy with the kindly thoughts you
 think
If you respect and treat him as your most important guest.
He will be grateful and your home will be forever blest.
And throughout the day and far into the night
The Christmas you dreamed of will be forever white.

With His Hand In Mine!

There are many doubting Thomases in the world
today . . . and all are ready to question the omnipotence of
God. . . .

A doubting Thomas may ask me how I know my Lord is
   real.
   He may doubt the things I say and doubt the way I
      feel.
But I know God's real today and He'll always be;
   I can feel His hand in mine, and, brother, that's
      enough for me!

Other friends that I love so—well, they may pass me by,
   Other friends may never see the teardrops in my eyes,
Other friends may never know the pain I bear,
   But God wipes away my every tear and every
      heartache shares.
               SO I KNOW
That I will never walk alone. Because He holds my hand
   And He will guide each step I take and if I fall I know
      He'll understand.
And when that time shall come to leave this world behind
   I shall walk that lonesome valley with His hand in
      mine!

Crowded World

We are living in a crowded and congested world. The football stadium, the racetracks, the theater, ticket counters at the airport, the streets, roads, and highways give us a feeling of being boxed in. However, I don't know of many churches that are overcrowded. But a lot of times it depends on whom you are with. There are some people you would like to be with regardless of the size of the crowd. To me that one is Jesus. I can enthusiastically say and sing to him:

> I'll always want to be with you,
> Amid the crowd or all alone.
> Because it's you and only you
> Who makes my life a lovely song!

How about you?

I Depend on Him

Everyone at some time or other has a few trials and tribulations. To some this occurs often, others not so often, some big, some small. Some seek advice and comfort from friends, lawyers, relatives, bankers, doctors, ministers, psychiatrists, *et al*. I have had my days of anxiety, discouragement, depressed feelings, burdens I thought I could not bear. But one day I found the answer to my feelings of despondency, the solution to my problem. It changed my life completely. The answer is found in one of the songs I have written.

> When the storm clouds gather round,
> And my world is tumbling down,
> When my day is filled with fear,
> And my load I cannot bear,
>
> Then to my Lord I go
> Because He loves me so.
> So I depend on Him
> Every day in every way!

It works for me! I feel sure it will work for you. Try it!

Teach Me, Lord

One day I was walking down the Kings Highway and I saw the footprints of Jesus and in the distance the old rugged Cross. I realized the excruciating pain and suffering he must have experienced as he hung on the cross. And he did it because he loves us. When I awoke, I was not the same man who had gone asleep. I got up immediately and wrote the following song:

> When I wake up in the morning
> To face another day,
> I whisper to the Master,
> "Please have Thine own way."
> Teach me, Lord, and lead me.
> Hold me by my hand.
> Only you can lead me to
> the Promised Land."

Singing that song each morning before I go to work, to church, or to other various and sundry activities has become my daily habit.

The Handicapped and God

There are many handicapped persons in the world today. This may be because of accidents, birth defects, or complications that took place in later years. Unfortunately, there are many people who look upon crippled or otherwise handicapped people as a nuisance and don't want to have anything to do with them. However, many companies employ them. But many don't think that the handicapped can do any kind of work and don't want them around.

Recently, I was listening to a telethon, and none of the performers who sang had any song that was related to the people for whom the telethon was being done. As I listened, a thought occurred to me. So I sat there in front of the TV and wrote a song regarding people who are handicapped. The following is one of the verses:

> He may be handicapped.
> He may be torn with pain.
> Still he is a child of God,
> Who loves him just the same.

What do you think?

Walking with God

There are many roads, paths, and highways in life. Many are marked with Go, Caution, Stop. We go over these trails alone, sometimes in a crowd. We ask ourselves many times, "Where does this road, trail, or highway lead?" When we get on dangerous paths, we sometimes wish we had someone to talk with us and walk or ride with us and show us the way. There is someone who can do just that, whether it be a path, trail, or highway or the road that leads to eternity.

> Sometimes I walk in the shadows.
> Sometimes in sunlight clear;
> But whether in gloom or darkness
> My Lord is always near.
>
> He walks with me, and he talks with me
> As he holds me by my hand.
> It is good to know that my Lord
> Is someone who understands.

Whatever your destination, it would be safer to have God walking or riding with you.